BEGINNINGS

PLANTS

ORIGINS AND EVOLUTION

EVOLUTION OF THE UNIVERSE

4.5 billion years ago the oceans and first landmasses form.

9

1 million years after the Big Bang, hydrogen atoms form.

5

10-20 billion years ago, in less than a second, four things happen.

1. The Big Bang
2. Inflation
3. The beginning of the four forces
4. The first atomic nuclei form

1 billion years after the Big Bang, galaxies begin to form.

6

8   4.6 billion years ago the Earth's crust forms.

7   5 billion years ago the planet Earth forms.

11   2.5 billion years ago the atmosphere forms.

10   3 billion years ago bacteria appear— life begins.

BEGINNINGS

PLANTS
ORIGINS AND EVOLUTION

by
Alessandro Garassino

English Translation by Rocco Serini

RSVP

**RAINTREE
STECK-VAUGHN**
P U B L I S H E R S
The Steck-Vaughn Company

Austin, Texas

Published by Raintree Steck-Vaughn Publishers, an imprint of Steck-Vaughn Company

Series Editor: Caterina Longanesi
American Edition, Edit and Rewrite: Susan Wilson
Consultant: Thomas R. Meagher, Director, Program of Ecology and Evolution, Rutgers University
Project Manager: Julie Klaus
Electronic Production: Scott Melcer
Cover Artwork: Marco Rosso and Isabella Salmoirago

Photographs DAVIDE CERIOLI, Nicorvo, Pavia: p. 37 (2). ALBERTO CONTRI, Milan: p. 8 (2), p. 16 (2), p. 33 (7, 8), p. 37 (4, 5). TONY CRADDOCK/GRAZIA NERI, Milan: p. 27 (4). RAFFAELE FATONE, Province of Borromeo, Milan: p. 9 (4, 5), p. 41 (5). ALESSAN-DRO GARASSINO, Milan: p. 40 (2). Editoriale Jaca Book, Milan (Carlo Scotti): p. 13 (4), p. 15 (3), p. 17 (5, 6), p. 21 (4), p. 25 (5, 7), p. 26 (1, 2, 3), p. 29 (5), p. 30 (1, 2, 3), p. 32 (2), p. 34 (1), p. 35 (3). JOHN G. MORRIS/W. EUGENE SMITH: p. 27 (5). GIOVANNI PINNA, Milan: p. 14 (1), p. 20 (2), p. 38 (1). MADALENA POCCIANTI, Scandicci, Florence: p. 17 (4). FABIO TERRANEO, Giussano, Milan: p. 39 (3). GIORGIO TERUZZI, Milan: p. 7 (3), p. 12 (3), p. 20 (1), p. 21 (3), p. 24 (1, 3), p. 34 (2).

Illustrations Editoriale Jaca Book, Milan (Cesare Dattena): p. 46-47; (Rosalba Moriggia and Maria Piatto): p. ii, p.iii, p. 8 (1), p. 10, p. 12 (stages), p. 17 (3), p. 28 (1, 2), p. 29 (3, 4), p. 31, p. 32 (1), p. 35 (4), p. 36 (1), p. 38 (2), p. 39 (4); (Lorenzo Orlandi): p. 12 (1); (Marco Rosso and Isabella Salmoirago): p. 19 (1), p. 22.
Illustrations p. 32 (3, 4, 5, 6), p. 33 (9, 10, 11), p. 40 (1, 3), p. 41 (4) are taken from *Flore Complète Illustrée en Couleurs de France, Suisse et Belgique* by Gaston Bonnor and Robert Douin, illustrated by Julie Poinsot, 13 vol., Librairie Générale de l'Enseignement Paris 1911-1935, republished in 2 vol. by Editions Belin, Paris 1990 (ediz. Ital. Editoriale Jaca Book, Milan 1990).
Illustration p. 12 (2), p. 13 (5), p. 14 (2), p. 16 (1), p. 18 (2, 3, 4, 5), p. 24 (2, 4, 6, 8), p. 31 (Archaeosperma) are from *Paleobotany and the Evolution of Plants* by Wilson N. Stewart, professor emeritus of Botany at University of Alberta, Edmonton, Canada, published by Cambridge University Press, Cambridge-New York-Melbourne 1983.

Graphics and Layout: The Graphics Department of Jaca Book
Special thanks to the Museum of Natural History of Milan

Library of Congress Cataloging-in-Publication Data
Garassino, Alessandro.
   [Piante. English]
   Plants: origins and evolution / Alessandro Garassino.
      p.   cm. — (Beginnings)
   Includes index.
   ISBN 0-8114-3332-3
   1. Plants — Evolution — Juvenile literature. 2. Botany — Juvenile literature.
[1. Plants, Fossil. 2. Evolution. 3. Botany.] I. Title. II. Series: Beginnings (Austin, Tex.)
QK980.G3713 1995
581.3'8—dc20   94-3838
                                                    CIP
                                                     AC

Printed and bound in the United States

1 2 3 4 5 6 7 8 9 0 KP 99 98 97 96 95 94

TABLE OF CONTENTS

THE PLANT KINGDOM

When you walk through a garden, a forest, or even a vacant lot, you see many different kinds of plants. Some are tall and have thick, woody stems. Others may be very small and grow along the ground with soft stems and colorful flowers. Some have needle-like leaves, while others have thick, fleshy leaves.

The great variety of plant life is a result of evolution, the process in which organisms change from one generation to the next. After major changes, some members of a species can evolve, or change into a new species. In this way, life started with very simple living things that evolved over time into the great variety of organisms we find today.

Although we cannot directly observe evolution, we can learn much from studying fossils, the remains or traces of organisms that lived in the past. Using fossils we can discover which organisms lived during the many ages of the Earth. We can trace how various organisms survived without change, died out, or changed over time.

1. Complex plants that we find today evolved from simpler organisms. The first organisms, bacteria and blue-green bacteria, evolved during the Precambrian Era, more than 3 billion years ago. Algae, which belong to the protist kingdom, evolved later and led to the evolution of the plant kingdom.

There is a great variety of stems, leaves, flowers, and fruit in the plant kingdom which can be seen in the **(2)** baobab, **(3)** ferns, **(4)** capers, and **(5)** elderberry.

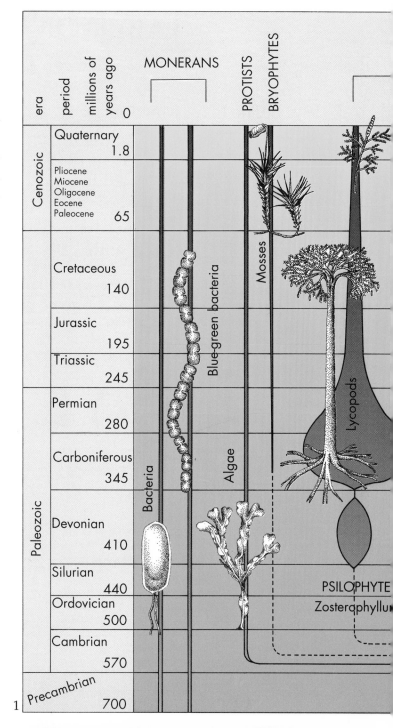

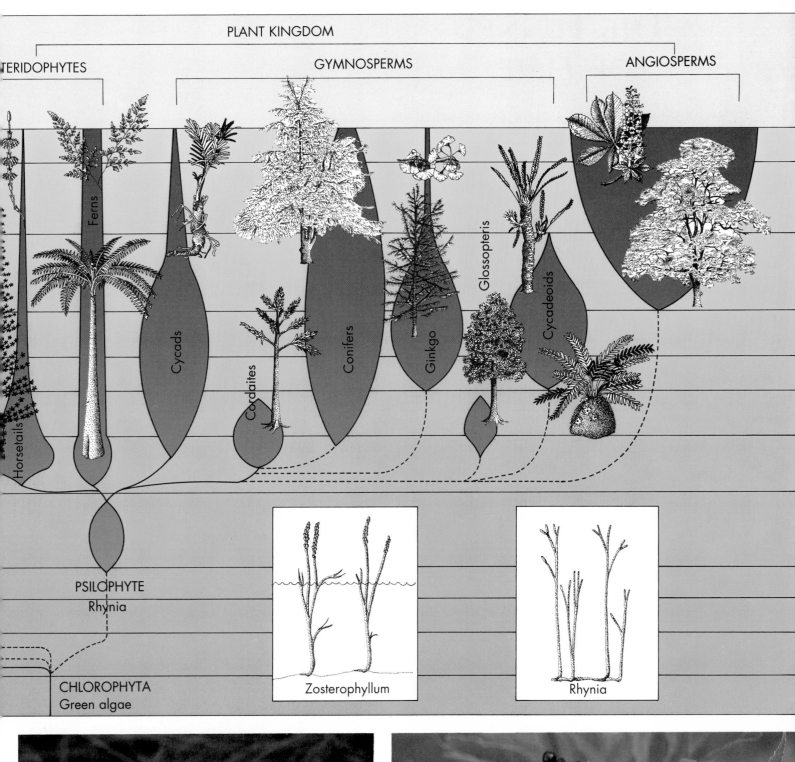

PLANT KINGDOM

TERIDOPHYTES   GYMNOSPERMS   ANGIOSPERMS

Ferns

Horsetails

Cycads

Cordaites

Conifers

Ginkgo

Glossopteris

Cycadeoids

PSILOPHYTE
Rhynia

CHLOROPHYTA
Green algae

Zosterophyllum

Rhynia

4

5

THE TUNNEL OF TIME

By carefully examining ancient fossils, scientists have found that life on Earth began more than 3.5 billion years ago. Very simple types of organisms that are still abundant today, bacteria and blue-green bacteria, were among the first living things. Blue-green bacteria, also called cyanobacteria, are

PTERIDOPHYTES
seedless vascular
plants
350

PSILOPHYTES
primitive vascular
plants
410

BACTERIA
BLUE-GREEN
BACTERIA
monerans
3,500

ALGAE
single-celled
and multicellular
organisms
2,500

millions of years ago

photosynthetic. Like plants they make their own food using carbon dioxide and give off oxygen as a waste product. This release of oxygen had a profound effect on the Earth. It formed the beginning of the oxygen-rich **atmosphere** that would eventually support a variety of plants and animals.

From the blue-green bacteria another more complex organism evolved—a simple green alga called Chlorophyta. Like the bacteria, this alga is single-celled, but the organization within its cells is much more complex. Chlorophyta cells were a springboard for all types of plant evolution. Large, multicellular algae evolved from green alga, as did different types of plants that live on land.

The first plants were very small, multicellular organisms that could only live in very damp areas. From these evolved a simple type of fern, the psilophytes. There are only two surviving species of psilophytes—one of these is the whisk fern. Gymnosperms and **angiosperms**, the most common plants today, evolved from early psilophytes.

GYMNOSPERMS
flowerless
seed plants
345

ANGIOSPERMS
flowering
seed plants
140

11

THE FIRST FORMS OF LIFE

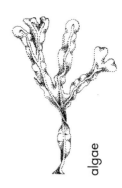

bacteria and blue-green bacteria

algae

The first things to live on Earth were monerans, simple one-celled organisms that lack a nucleus or any other organization within the cells. As you know, bacteria, which are monerans, are still common today. Although the world is teeming with bacteria, one type is found only in sulfur-rich, hot pools, an environment in which few other organisms can live. These bacteria get energy from the hot water and need no oxygen to survive. Instead they use hydrogen sulfide (the compound responsible for the smell of rotten eggs) to make their own food. Hydrogen sulfide is a major gas given off by volcanoes and was probably very common in the Earth's early atmosphere.

At some point, blue-green bacteria evolved. Like plants, they could make food by photosynthesis and needed carbon dioxide and light, as well as water and oxygen. As the blue-green bacteria became more numerous, they gave off so much oxygen that they changed the atmosphere. After a while, sulfur-dependent bacteria could not survive in the changed environment.

Blue-green bacteria are found today in fresh as well as salt water, often living in colonies. Unlike the blue-green, other types of bacteria cannot perform photosynthesis. Many of these bacteria do not live in water. Some need oxygen; others can live without it. But all types of bacteria have common features. They are very simple, single-celled, microscopic organisms surrounded by a **cell** wall. Within their single cell, there are no organelles, or structures that are found in more complex organisms. Bacterial cells may be spherical, rod-shaped, or spiral-shaped. And some types of bacterial cells may be linked together in clumps or in long chains.

Fossils of ancient bacteria have been found in Canada, South Africa, and Australia. Studies have been done on fossils like *Ainimikiea*, *Archaeonema*, and *Palaeolyngbya*. These have shown that the ancient forms are very similar to the bacteria and blue-green bacteria of today.

1

2 3

psilophytes

pteridophytes

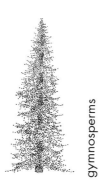
gymnosperms

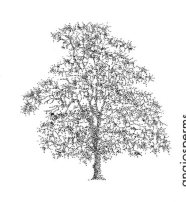
angiosperms

4

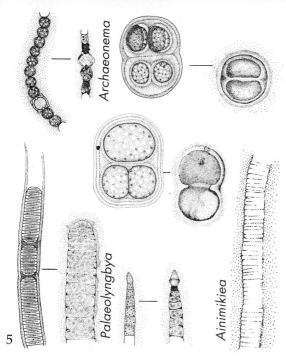

Archaeonema

Palaeolyngbya

Ainimikiea

5

1. An artist's concept of bacterial cells in the primordial seas.
2. *Gunflintia*, a fossil similar to bacteria common today, found in Gunflint Formation, Canada.
3. These stromatolites living in Shark Bay, Australia, are similar to those that lived billions of years ago. Stromatolites are thick mats of bacteria, blue-green bacteria, and sand. The mats build up as sand adheres to a sticky substance given off by the organisms. When the bacteria are covered by sand, they move up through the sand and again attract more sand. In this way they form new layers and large structures.
4. Sections of stromatolite fossils. *Collenia nudosa*, on the left, was found in Minnesota. A different type of stromatolite from Cochabamba, Bolivia, is shown on the right. Both fossils belong to the Precambrian Era and are about 2 billion years old.
5. These pairs of blue-green bacteria show that they have changed very little over time. Blue-green bacteria found today (on the left side of each pair) are similar to their fossil ancestors (shown on the right).

ALGAE

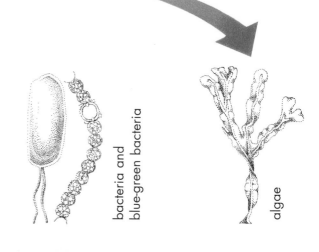

bacteria and blue-green bacteria

algae

At one time the blue-green bacteria were classified as algae. Like algae, the blue-green bacteria are photosynthetic—they make their own food in the presence of light. They also share common traits such as having a cell wall and having **chlorophyll**, the pigment needed for photosynthesis. But unlike algae, the blue-green bacteria do not have a nucleus or other organelles, the structures within the cell. Because this simple structure makes blue-green bacteria more similar to other monerans than to algae, they have been reclassified as monerans.

Other organisms classified as algae have also undergone a name change. In the past, algae were classified as plants. But as research equipment and techniques have improved, scientists have concluded that algae are more similar to other protists than to plants. Now all algae, unicellular as well as very large organisms, are classified as protists.

The first algae may have appeared about 2.5 billion years ago during the Precambrian Era. At this time there was enough oxygen in the water to support their growth. An early type of algae, the Chlorophyta, or green algae, is believed to be the ancestor of all modern plants. Although some of the present-day green algae may measure more than 20 feet long, the first ones were probably tiny unicellular organisms. Many modern species are also unicellular and live in fresh or salt water.

As algae evolved they gained the ability to reproduce sexually. This brought variation in new generations and made possible a great diversity of life forms. Some simpler algae evolved into the many divisions of algae living today. These include the giant kelps and other brown algae, as well as the red algae which include most types of seaweeds. Other adaptations gave rise to new species of plants which could live on land.

1

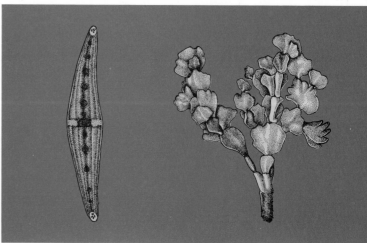

2

psilophytes

pteridophytes

gymnosperms

angiosperms

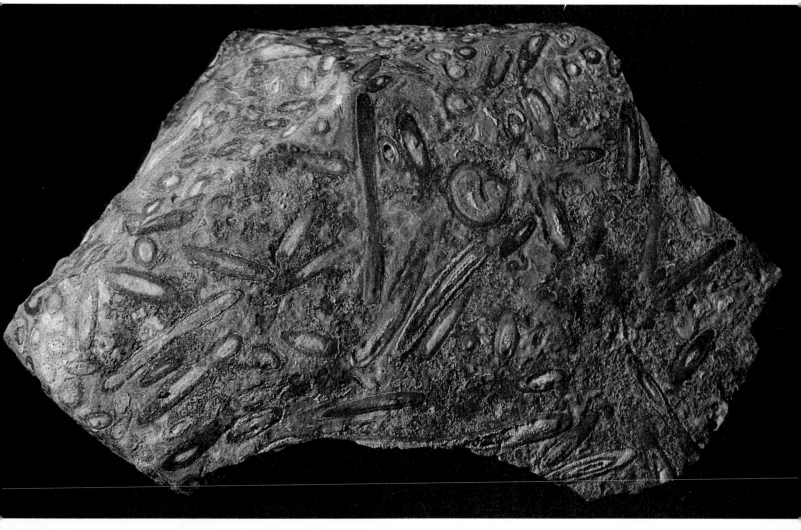

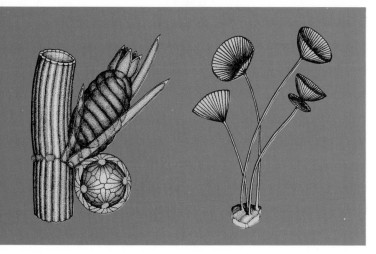

1. *Fucus vesiculosus*, a brown algae found living off the coasts of the United States and other temperate waters.
2. Algae include *Closterium, Halimeda, Chara,* and *Acetabularia.*
3. Fossils of *Diplopora annulata* were found in a rock from Italy. These fossils are believed to be from the Triassic Period about 200 million years ago.

INVADERS OF THE LAND

Life began in water billions of years ago. Water not only provided organisms with nutrients, it also protected them from drying out. In addition water helped organisms to reproduce. It moved sex cells together and allowed new organisms to form.

More than 400 million years ago the first living things moved out of the ocean and onto land. Here plants found plenty of carbon dioxide and sunshine, both needed for photosynthesis. They also had less competition than in the now-swarming waters. But after moving onto land, plants needed to adapt to several challenges. They needed to move nutrients to all parts of the plant, support large tissues, reproduce out of water, and avoid drying out. Plant evolution was a directed movement toward meeting the challenges of living on land.

Fossils of some of the first types of plants can be found in many parts of the world, including the United States, Canada, and England. Evidence of some plants show up in the Silurian Period about 420 million years ago. Fossils of many more types of complex plants can be found from the Devonian Period, about 395 million years ago.

One of the oldest fossil plants is *Cooksonia*, which was about 2.5 inches tall. It vanished without leaving any descendants. Most modern plants are believed to have evolved from two similar psilophytes that lived during the Devonian Period. One plant, *Zosterophyllum*, was about 8 inches tall, with thin stems and branches. Lycopods evolved from this plant. The club mosses that have survived today are an example of a lycopod. The other ancient plant was *Rhynia*, a reedlike plant about 6 inches tall. Our ferns, horsetails, gymnosperms, and angiosperms came from *Rhynia*.

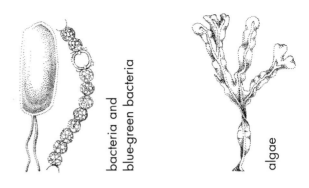

bacteria and blue-green bacteria

algae

1. A swamp in the Devonian Period, about 400 million years ago, may have looked something like the artist's reconstruction. The plants were relatively primitive, many of them having branched stems but no leaves. Plants shown from left to right are *Zosterophyllum rehenanum*, *Asteroxylon mackiei*, and *Rhynia major*.

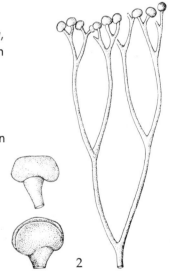

2. The oldest known vascular plant, *Cooksonia calendonica*, lived at the end of the Silurian Period, about 420 million years ago. The reproductive organ, which contained spores, is shown at the left.
3., 4., 5. Plants of the Devonian Period, shown from left to right are *Zosterophyllum rehenanum*, *Asteroxylon mackiei*, and *Psilophyton dawsonii*.

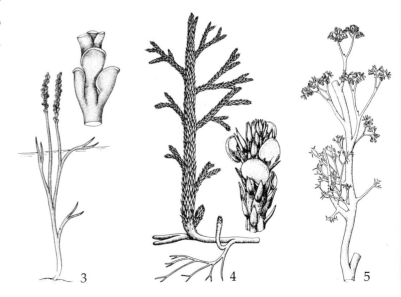

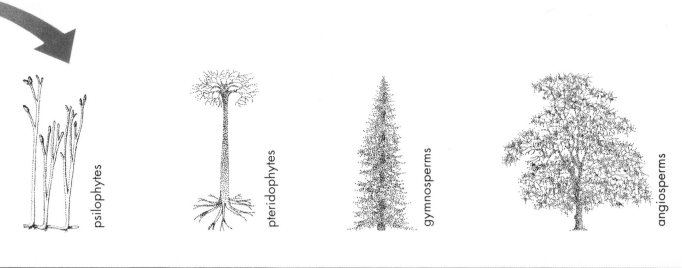

psilophytes

pteridophytes

gymnosperms

angiosperms

1

BRYOPHYTES AND VASCULAR PLANTS

Not long after plants moved onto land, they evolved into at least two separate groups—the bryophytes and the vascular plants. Bryophytes are relatively small, simple plants that have no special tissues to circulate materials throughout the plant. So water moves slowly through this type of plant, from one cell to the next. Because of this, a bryophyte is limited in size—it simply cannot carry water more than a certain distance. Most are also limited to living in very moist areas.

Bryophyte fossils have been found as early as the Devonian Period, and some very closely resemble bryophytes living today. Modern bryophytes include the mosses, liverworts, and hornworts.

The other major group of land plants are the vascular plants. In contrast to bryophytes, vascular plants have specialized tissues which carry materials throughout the plant. The tissues make up tubes that carry water and food. This system of tubes is comparable to your blood system, which quickly carries fluids to all parts of your body. Vascular tissue is an adaptation that makes these plants successful, allowing them to grow into tall trees and to live far from the water's edge.

Vascular plants soon evolved specialized organs—roots, leaves, and stems. True roots grew down into the soil, anchoring the plant and taking in water and nutrients. Leaves were the main organs of photosynthesis. Stems, which were already present in more primitive plants, connected the other organs. These stems supported the plants, growing thick with vascular tissue and holding leaves up to the sunlight.

Fossils of the earliest vascular plants are about 400 million years old. Some of the most impressive fossils of ancient vascular plants can be found in petrified forests. Here plant tissue has been replaced over time by minerals, forming trees of stone.

1. The moss *Sporogonites exuberans* lived during the Devonian Period, about 400 million years ago. Thin stems were topped with reproductive organs.
2. Present-day mosses live close to the ground and are similar in structure to ancient forms.

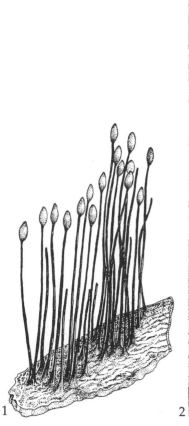

1

2

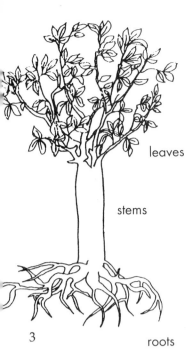

leaves

stems

3

roots

4

5

3. Vascular plants have evolved true roots, stems, and leaves.

4. Petrified logs cover the ground in Petrified Forest National Park, Arizona.

5. A section of a petrified log shows structures present when the tree was alive. As the tree decayed, mineral-filled water seeped into its cells. The log is now made up largely of quartz. The red areas of the rock are formed by iron oxides.

6. This fossilized trunk shows details of the decayed tree from which it formed.

6

CARBONIFEROUS FORESTS

During the Carboniferous Period, from about 345 to 280 million years ago, the Earth's **climate** was generally warm and moist. Today's temperate regions of North America and Europe had tropical or even subtropical climates. Plants flourished in this environment. Pteridophytes, the seedless vascular plants, reached great heights. Vascular tissue allowed the plants to grow tall. The taller a plant grew, the less competition it had for sunlight and the farther it could spread its spores from which new plants would grow. Great swamp forests covered much of the land, filled with giant tree ferns, lycopod trees, and horsetails.

bacteria and blue-green bacteria

algae

Although club mosses found today are very small, the Carboniferous forests were dominated by the closely-related, giant lycopod trees. The most numerous lycopod was the *Lepidodendron*, which grew up to 130 feet tall. *Sigillaria*, another lycopod, grew up to 65 feet tall. These giant lycopods are now extinct.

Horsetails were another tree in the swamp forests of the Carboniferous Period. One type, *Calamites*, grew up to 33 feet tall. Although horsetails can still be found today, they are all small plants. The horsetail species that grew into tree-sized plants are now extinct.

Tree ferns are the only giant survivors of the seedless vascular plants. Although the tree-sized ferns are usually found only in tropical forests, smaller ferns can be found in most parts of the world. During the Carboniferous Period, *Psaronius* grew to about 10 feet tall.

In addition to the seedless giants, gymnosperms could also be found in the Carboniferous swamp forests. One gymnosperm, *cordaitales*, which grew to 130 feet tall, is now extinct.

Fossils of giant horsetails of the Carboniferous Period.
1. Foliage of *Annularia*.
2., 3. Fragments of the trunks of *Calamites*.
4. Foliage of *Annularia*, found in Mazon Creek, Illinois.

1

2

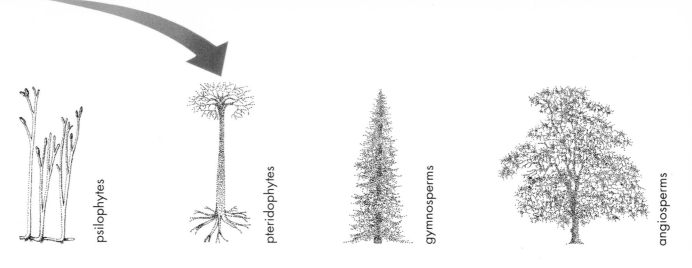

psilophytes

pteridophytes

gymnosperms

angiosperms

Artist's reconstruction of a Carboniferous forest 345 million years ago. The dominant trees in the forest were the giant lycopods, *Lepidodendron* and *Sigillaria*. Giant horsetails, such as *Calamites*, and tree ferns, such as *Psaronius*, were also present.

A few gymnosperms, such as *Cordaites* and *Medullosa*, could also be found. A variety of large insects swarmed through the trees. And the first reptiles, such as the 8-inch long *Hylonomus* appeared.

3

4

S&r '93

FOSSILS OF THE CARBONIFEROUS PERIOD

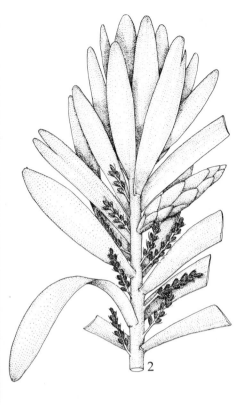

1. Fragment of a fossil trunk of *Cordaites*, found in Germany. This fossil is about 345 million years old, from the Carboniferous Period.
2. *Cordaites* had long, lance-shaped leaves and shoots extending from the branches.
3. This fossil of a fernlike plant is from the Carboniferous Period and was found in Illinois.
4. *Medullosa* was a fernlike tree that had seeds and was one of the earliest gymnosperms. The insets at the base of the tree show the cross sections of a branch. The inset on the left shows two tubes of vascular tissue. The inset on the right shows several tubes and wide area to which leaves were attached

1

2

3

4

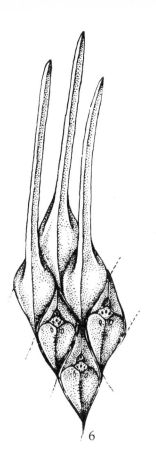

6

Two treelike lycopods of
the Carboniferous Period.
5. Section of *Lepidodendron*
showing leaves and leaf scars.
6. Fossils of the *Lepidodendron*
show diamond-shaped leaf scars
that formed as each leaf broke
off the trunk.
7. Leaf scars of *Sigillaria*.
8. Fragments of a fossil trunk of
Sigillaria showing six-sided leaf
scars.

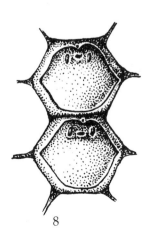

8

5

7

COAL DEPOSITS

It's hard to imagine that forests that evolved, grew, and died out hundreds of millions of years ago could still be important to people. But the forests of the Carboniferous Period are very important to us today. They are the source of fossil fuels—coal, petroleum, and natural gas.

Plants living in the swamp forests of the Carboniferous Period were tall but shallow-rooted. They were easily uprooted in strong winds. Often the trees would totally sink into the marshy ground before they had completely decomposed. Covered by sediment, the partially decayed trees turned into a spongy substance called peat. When the peat was later covered by sedimentary rock, the peat was compressed. In time, and with the proper conditions, such as temperature, the peat turned into coal. The first type of coal to form is called lignite, a relatively soft coal. After a longer period of time, lignite can change into **bituminous coal**, and finally into **anthracite**, the oldest, hardest, and most valuable coal.

1

3

2

4

5

1. Anthracite coal, the oldest type, is hard and black. It formed during the Paleozoic Era.
2. Bituminous coal is softer than anthracite and formed during the Paleozoic, Mesozoic, and Cenozoic eras.
3. Peat formed during the Cenozoic Era.
4. Strip mining is a way of extracting large amounts of coal. This mine, which covers an area of about 2 square miles, yields up to 140,000 cubic yards of coal per day. The excavator is so large that it had to be built on-site and took 2 years to build.
5. Unlike strip mining, mines such as this one in South Wales do not destroy the countryside. However, they are dangerous places to work. Miners may be trapped in collapsing mines, and they often die of lung disease caused by coal dust.

IN THE PERMIAN, PLANTS WERE DIFFERENT

Following the Carboniferous Period was the Permian Period. It was a time of great change lasting from about 280 to 245 million years ago. By about 280 million years ago, all the continents on Earth had moved together to form one massive continent called Pangea. As the continents moved, their climates changed. Land that had once been covered by lush forests became drier and colder. The pteridophytes, the giant horsetails, tree ferns, and lycopods that had dominated the forests of the Carboniferous Period, began to die out.

Taking the place of the pteridophytes were seed plants, which began to appear during the Carboniferous Period. As plants moved from water to land, a major problem was reproducing out of the water. Seeds were much better adapted to this than were the spores of non-seed plants. So seed plants had a major advantage when the climate became drier, and they began to dominate the northern part of Pangea.

In the Southern Hemisphere, where the climate was colder, vast forests grew up. Dominating these forests was a gymnosperm called *Glossopteris*, which is now extinct. This tree grew to a height of about 20 feet and had long, lance-shaped leaves. Fossils of these leaves have been found in places as far away from each other as South America and Australia, South Africa, and Antarctica. Finding these fossils in such widely separated areas helps support the theory that the continents had at one time been joined together.

1. During the Carboniferous Period, about 345 million years ago, the continents were widely spaced around the Earth.
2. The continents began to move together and formed a single large continent during the Permian Period, about 280 million years ago. The newly formed continent, Pangea, had two main parts—Laurasia in the north and Gondwana in the south.

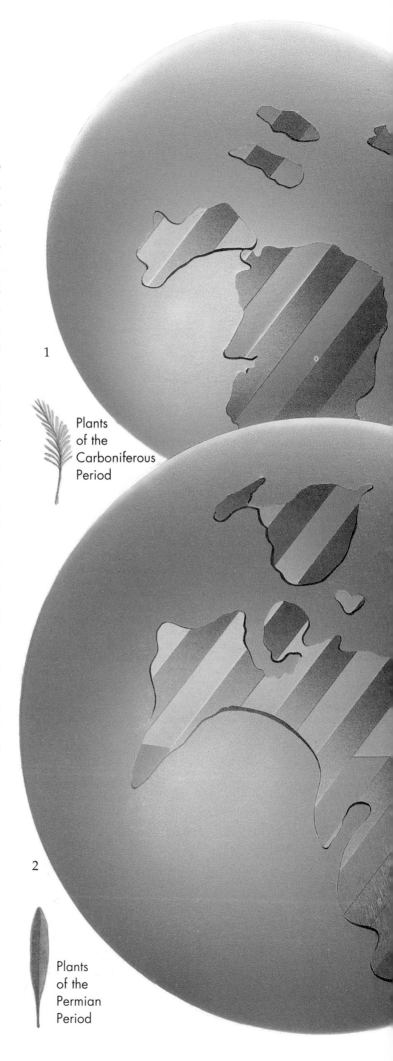

1

Plants of the Carboniferous Period

2

Plants of the Permian Period

3. The dominant plant in Gondwana throughout the Permian Period was the *Glossopteris*.
4. The large leaf of *Glossopteris* was lance-shaped and had parallel veins.
5. Fossils from Australia showing the typical lance-shaped leaf of *Glossopteris*.

5

3

4

GYMNOSPERMS

bacteria and
blue-green bacteria

algae

1

When plants first moved from water to land, they did not move very far. The first land plants lived near the ocean or in marshy areas. Once on land, they gradually adapted to being out of the water. One of the first adaptations was a cuticle, a waterproof coating that kept the plant from drying out. Once they were waterproofed, plants needed a way to absorb and transport water. True roots, which could absorb water, and vascular tissue, which carried the water to all parts, adapted the plant to this new need. After this adaptation there was one remaining challenge—the need to form new plants without being in water. Seed plants met this challenge. Seeds allowed plants to sexually reproduce without a constant source of water. You will learn more about seeds in the next chapter.

The first type of seed plants was the gymnosperm. Fossils from an early type of gymnosperm, *Archaeosperma*, have been found in Scotland and are believed to be from the end of the Devonian Period, about 345 million years ago. Many more gymnosperm fossils have been found from the Carboniferous Period.

1. The two parts of this fossil show the mold and cast of a pine cone from the Miocene Epoch, about 26 million years ago.

2., 3. Fossil imprints of branches of the monkey-puzzle tree from the Cretaceous Period, about 136 million years ago.

2

psilophytes

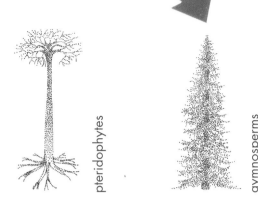
pteridophytes

gymnosperms

angiosperms

sori

spore

spore case

fern

Ferns reproduce by means of spores, which develop within spore cases called sori. After a spore is released, it develops into a separate, tiny plant that produces sperm and eggs. The sperm and egg need water in order to unite and grow into the typical fern plant.

The egg and sperm of seed plants unite on the parent plant where there is water and the embryo is protected. The gymnosperm *Archaeosperma* has an expanded stemlike structure that protects the seed.

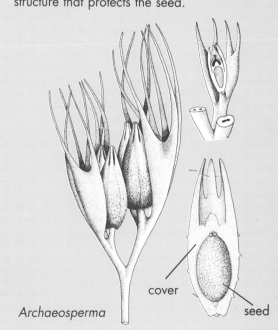

cover

seed

Archaeosperma

3

SEEDS

The seedless vascular plants used spores for sexual reproduction. But spores need water to form a new plant. Without a constant source of water, they easily dry out. Lacking enough rainfall, or some other source of water, this type of plant could not sexually reproduce.

Seed plants were a giant evolutionary step. In these plants the female sex cell remained attached to the plant. Once the male sex cell united with it, the embryo of a new plant could develop, protected by the parent plant. The embryo and additional food were encased in a hard, waterproof covering and then shed from the plant. This little package, the seed, could then develop into a new plant when conditions were right. If the ground was hard and dry, or if it was too cold, nothing would happen to the seed. Only when rain and warmth arrived did the seed sprout and begin to grow. This makes seed plants more adaptable than non-seed plants to changing weather. Thus the first seed plants, gymnosperms, were at an advantage when the climate changed during the Permian Period.

wing

embryo

endosperm

1. Section of a seed with a large wing attached. The wing is easily lifted by the wind, helping to scatter seeds far from the parent plant. The embryo inside the seed will develop into a young plant when conditions are right. While the embryo grows and before the young plant is able to make its own food, nutrients will be supplied by the endosperm.
2. Pine cone fossils of *Araucaria mirabilis*, from the Jurassic Period, about 170 million years ago.

3. *Larix europaea* pine cones.
4. *Abies pectinata* pine cone.
5. *Pinus pinea* pine cone.
6. *Pinus maritima* pine cone.
7. Larch.
8. Fir trees.
9. *Pinus halepensis*.
10. *Abies pectinata*.
11. *Pinus cembra*.

33

LIVING FOSSILS

Charles Darwin, the father of the theory of evolution, coined the phrase *living fossil* to describe the ginkgo. This tree had survived, almost unchanged, from ancient times. Darwin and other scientists have found many additional living fossils, both plant and animal, that have undergone little change for hundreds of millions of years.

Ginkgo biloba was originally found in temple gardens in East Asia. It is now commonly planted in the United States and much of the rest of the world. The ginkgo is unusual in that unlike most other gymnosperms, it is not an evergreen. In fall the ginkgo's fan-shaped leaves turn bright yellow and drop from the tree.

Another type of gymnosperm that has survived with little change is the cycad. The *Cycas revoluta*, sometimes called the false palm, can be found in parks and gardens in the United States and Europe. Although cycads are not believed to be the oldest seed plants, they are the most primitive.

One other gymnosperm considered a living fossil is the giant sequoia tree. Giant sequoias may be the oldest, as well as some of the largest, living things on Earth. The General Sherman Tree in California is believed to be more than 2,000 years old. It measures 275 feet tall and over 100 feet around its base. Giant sequoias grow only in the Sierra Nevada Mountains of California.

1. Fan-shaped leaves of the *Ginkgo biloba*.
2. Although *Cycas revoluta* looks similar to palm trees, it is a cycad.
3. This rock found in the United States contains a ginkgo fossil and is thought to be from the Paleocene Epoch, about 60 million years ago.
4. The living fossils found today with their fossil ancestors. The three plants at the left are ferns, the four at the right are gymnosperms.

3

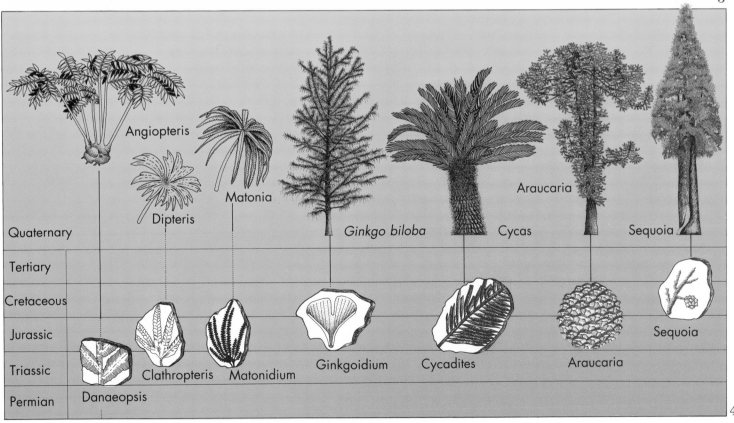

	Angiopteris					Araucaria	
Quaternary	Dipteris	Matonia	Ginkgo biloba	Cycas			Sequoia
Tertiary							
Cretaceous					Araucaria		Sequoia
Jurassic	Clathropteris	Matonidium	Ginkgoidium	Cycadites			
Triassic							
Permian	Danaeopsis						

4

35

The Flowering Plants — Angiosperms

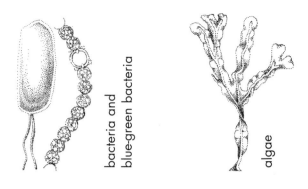

bacteria and
blue-green bacteria

algae

Throughout time, the world has changed, and living things have adapted to those changes. Those organisms that are the best adapted are the most successful. They are the most numerous and often the most diversified. In the beginning, the simplest organisms, bacteria, were the most successful. Much later was the age of the dinosaur, when those huge creatures roamed the Earth. Today could be called the age of the angiosperms. Angiosperms, or flowering plants, are everywhere. They are the roses in your garden, the grass on your lawn, the elm giving shade, the wheat in the fields, and even the broccoli on your plate.

Although these plants are referred to as flowering, angiosperms may have tiny, inconspicuous flowers. The flowers of an elm tree or a grass plant are neither large nor brightly colored. Colored flowers evolved as an adaptation which aids in pollination, or the transfer of pollen from male parts of a flower to female parts. The colorful petals, as well as sweet scents, attract insects and other animals. While gathering nectar, a bee will brush against pollen laden parts of a flower. Gathering more nectar, the bee will brush against the next flower, effectively spreading pollen from one flower to the next.

In addition to adapting flowers to attract animals, angiosperms have a basic adaptation not found in gymnosperms. Their seeds develop inside, and are protected by, a fruit. Angiosperms first evolved at the beginning of the Cretaceous Period, about 140 million years ago. Fossils of early angiosperms have been found in North and South America as well as in Europe and Africa.

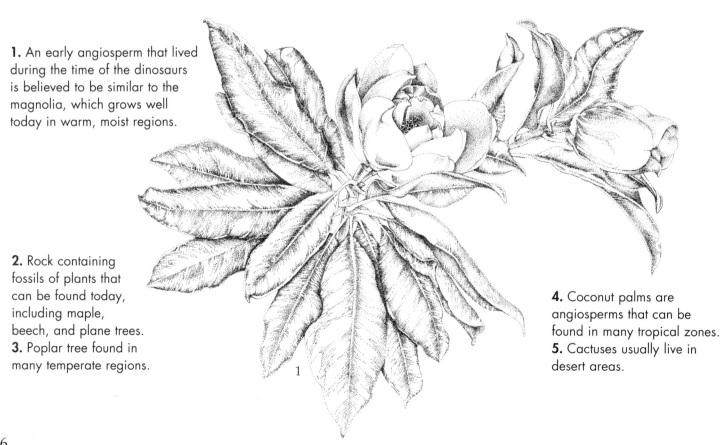

1. An early angiosperm that lived during the time of the dinosaurs is believed to be similar to the magnolia, which grows well today in warm, moist regions.

2. Rock containing fossils of plants that can be found today, including maple, beech, and plane trees.
3. Poplar tree found in many temperate regions.

1

4. Coconut palms are angiosperms that can be found in many tropical zones.
5. Cactuses usually live in desert areas.

psilophytes

pteridophytes

gymnosperms

angiosperms

3

2

4

5

FLOWERS

The flower is the reproductive organ of flowering plants. Complete flowers have both male and female parts—with the male stamen and the female pistil. The anther, at the tip of the stamen, produces and stores pollen, which contains the male sex cell. Pollen is moved, usually by wind or by insects, to the stigma, at the tip of the pistil. From the stigma, the male sex cell moves down the pistil to the female sex cell, which is inside the ovary at the base of the pistil. Here the two sex cells unite and form an embryo, a very early stage of a new plant. The embryo, plus stored food, is surrounded by a tough outer coat to make a seed.

1

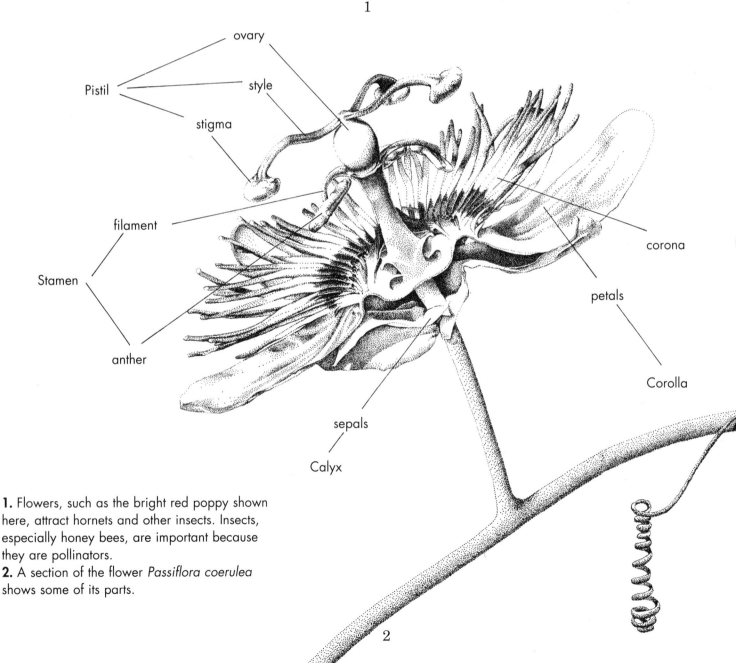

2

1. Flowers, such as the bright red poppy shown here, attract hornets and other insects. Insects, especially honey bees, are important because they are pollinators.
2. A section of the flower *Passiflora coerulea* shows some of its parts.

AND LEAVES

The leaves of most plants have two main functions. First, through tiny pores in the surface of the leaf, they release water from the plant in a process called transpiration. Because water is being removed by transpiration, more water is pulled up through the plant's vascular tissue, just as water is sucked through a straw.

The other main function of leaves is photosynthesis, a complex process in which sugar is formed from carbon dioxide and water. Chlorophyll, the pigment which makes plants green, absorbs energy from sunlight, which is needed in the chemical reaction. Oxygen is given off as a waste product.

3

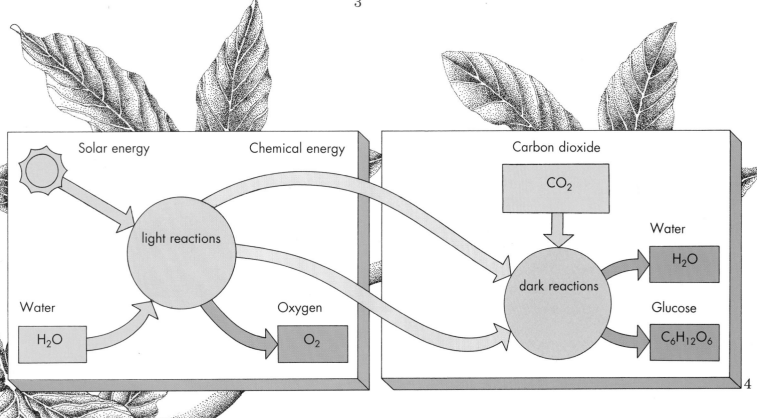

3. Foliage of *Helleborus lividus*, a plant typical of the island of Corsica.
4. The complex reactions of photosynthesis can be thought of as a two-step process. In the light reactions, sunlight is absorbed by the pigment, chlorophyll. The heat energy from sunlight is thus trapped and changed to chemical energy. That chemical energy splits water molecules and also supplies the energy needed for the reactions in the second step. During this step, called the dark reactions, carbon dioxide is combined with other carbon compounds and with hydrogen to form glucose. Oxygen is given off as a waste product. Glucose is a simple sugar which can be transformed by the plant into more complex sugars or into starch.

FRUIT

After seeds form in the ovary of a flower, the ovary enlarges and grows into a fruit. Fruit protects the seeds and may help scatter the seeds, as well. Some fruits break open when they ripen, and wind carries the seeds away. Other types of fruit are food for different animals. After the fruit is eaten, the seeds are usually passed out of the body into the soil far from the parent plant, where the seed will grow into a mature plant.

Botanists classify seeds into several types. Fleshy fruits are some of the most common fruits, such as peaches, cherries, or plums. **Aggregate** fruits, such as strawberries or blackberries, appear as a single fruit but are actually made up of many tiny fruits. Some other foods that we may not think of as fruits, such a peas, wheat, and poppies, are classified as dry fruits.

1. Blackberries *fruticosus* are an aggregate fruit, or collection of smaller fruits joined together.
2. Breadfruit grows on tall trees native to the Pacific Islands.
3. An apricot is an example of a fleshy fruit.
4. Grains are classified as dry fruits.
5. Chili peppers are the fruit of chili plants.

4

5

41

GLOSSARY

aggregate: A collection; in fruit, a collection of smaller fruit joined together.

angiosperm: A flowering seed plant.

anthracite: The oldest and hardest type of coal.

atmosphere: The gases that surround the Earth.

baobab: An African tree with a thick trunk and edible fruit.

bituminous coal: A form of coal harder and older than lignite, but softer and younger than anthracite.

bryophytes: Simple plants, such as mosses, that lack vascular tissue.

calyx: The outer leaflike parts of a flower that surround the petals.

caper: The edible flower bud of a low shrub.

carbon: An element found in all organic compounds, in many rocks, and in all living things. Carbon exists naturally in different forms such as diamonds and coal.

Carboniferous Period: A period of the Paleozoic Era when many coal beds formed.

cell: The basic unit of all living things.

chlorophyll: The green pigment, or coloring, contained in plants. Chlorophyll traps light and converts it into a form of energy that plants use to make food.

climate: The average weather in an area.

colony: A group of animals that live together and may build such structures as anthills or coral reefs.

conifer: The family of evergreen shrubs and trees that produce cones. Examples include pines, spruces, and firs.

corolla: The ring of petals, usually colored, that make up a flower.

Cretaceous Period: The third period of the Mesozoic Era.

Devonian Period: A period in the Paleozoic Era.

embryo: The earliest stage in the development of an organism.

endosperm: Food-storing tissue inside a seed.

era: A unit of geologic time which is subdivided into periods.

extinct: No longer living. Most species that have lived on Earth are now extinct.

fossil: The preserved remains or the trace of organisms that lived in the past.

genus: A grouping of closely related species.

gymnosperm: A plant whose seeds are not enclosed in a fruit.

kingdom: The largest classification division. The five kingdoms are monerans, protists, fungi, plants, and animals.

lignite: A soft brownish-black coal.

lycopods: Vascular plants that thrived as large trees during the Carboniferous Period. Club mosses are living examples of lycopods.

magnolia: A flowering shrub or tree with large, waxlike, fragrant flowers.

marsh: An area of wetland filled with plants.

monkey-puzzle: A Chilean pine tree.

moss: A simple nonvascular plant that often grows in tufts or clusters on decaying wood, the ground, or rocks.

organ: A part of an animal or plant that has a special function.

organism: A living thing.

ovary: In plants, a structure in which the female sex cells as well as the seeds develop.

oxygen: An odorless and colorless element found in air and water and needed by most living things.

peat: A partly decomposed, partially carbonized plant material used as a fuel for heating.

Permian Period: The last period of the Paleozoic Era.

photosynthesis: A process in which plants produce food using water and carbon dioxide in the presence of sunlight.

pigment: Organic coloring matter that gives animals and plants their color.

pistil: The female part of a flower.

pollen: Yellowish grains in seed plants that contain sperm.

pollination: The process in which pollen is carried from the male to the female parts of a plant.

psilophytes: Simple plants from which most modern plants are believed to have evolved.

pteridophytes: Vascular plants that reproduce by means of spores.

reproduction: The process by which living things produce their young.

sepal: One of the individual leaves of the calyx of a flower.

sequoia: A gigantic evergreen tree of the western United States, also called a giant redwood.

Silurian Period: A period of the Paleozoic Era.

sori: The tiny caplike structures made up of clusters of sporangia. Sori are found on the bottom of fern leaves.

species: The smallest classification group. A group of organisms that can interbreed and produce young that can also produce young.

sporangium: The plant structure that contains the spores.

spore: Structures given off by non-seed vascular plants which develop into a small plant where sexual reproduction takes place.

stamen: A male part of the flower.

stigma: The tip of the pistil.

stromatolites: An abundant fossil form produced by bacteria and blue-green bacteria.

style: The part of the pistil that connects the stigma and ovary.

tissue: A group of cells that have the same origin and the same functions in an organism.

transpiration: A process in which plants give off water into the atmosphere.

vascular tissue: Specialized tissue that moves materials, especially water, through a plant.

FURTHER READING

Behme, Robert L. *Incredible Plants: Oddities, Curiosities, and Eccentricities.* Sterling, 1992
Coil, Suzanne M. *Poisonous Plants.* Watts, 1992
Greenaway, Theresa. *The First Plants.* Raintree Steck-Vaughn, 1991
Greenaway, Theresa. *Mosses and Liverworts.* Raintree Steck-Vaughn, 1992
Johnson, Sylvia. *Mosses.* Lerner
Madgwick, Wendy. *Flowering Plants.* Raintree Steck-Vaughn, 1990
Margulis, Lynn. *Diversity of Life: The Five Kingdoms.* Enslow, 1992

INDEX

Evolution of the Moneran, Protist, Plant, and Fungi Kingdoms

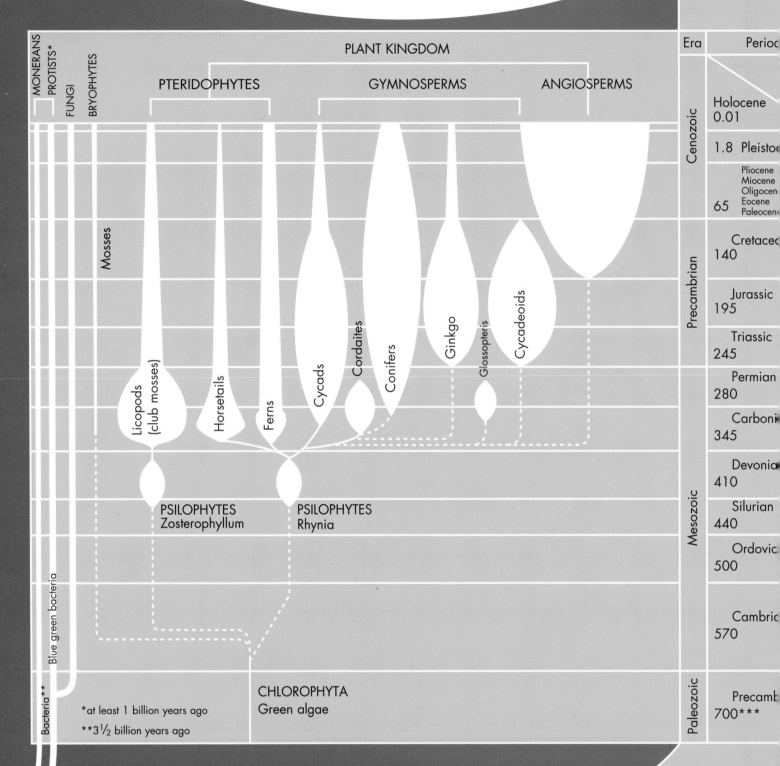

MONERANS

PROTISTS*

FUNGI

BRYOPHYTES

PLANT KINGDOM

PTERIDOPHYTES

GYMNOSPERMS

ANGIOSPERMS

Mosses

Licopods (club mosses)

Horsetails

Ferns

Cycads

Cordaites

Conifers

Ginkgo

Glossopteris

Cycadeoids

PSILOPHYTES
Zosterophyllum

PSILOPHYTES
Rhynia

Blue green bacteria

Bacteria**

CHLOROPHYTA
Green algae

*at least 1 billion years ago

**3½ billion years ago

Era	Period
Cenozoic	Holocene 0.01
	1.8 Pleistoc
	Pliocene Miocene Oligocen Eocene 65 Paleocen
Precambrian	Cretaced 140
	Jurassic 195
	Triassic 245
	Permian 280
	Carboni 345
Mesozoic	Devonia 410
	Silurian 440
	Ordovic 500
	Cambri 570
Paleozoic	Precamb 700***

EVOLUTION OF THE PROTIST AND ANIMAL KINGDOMS

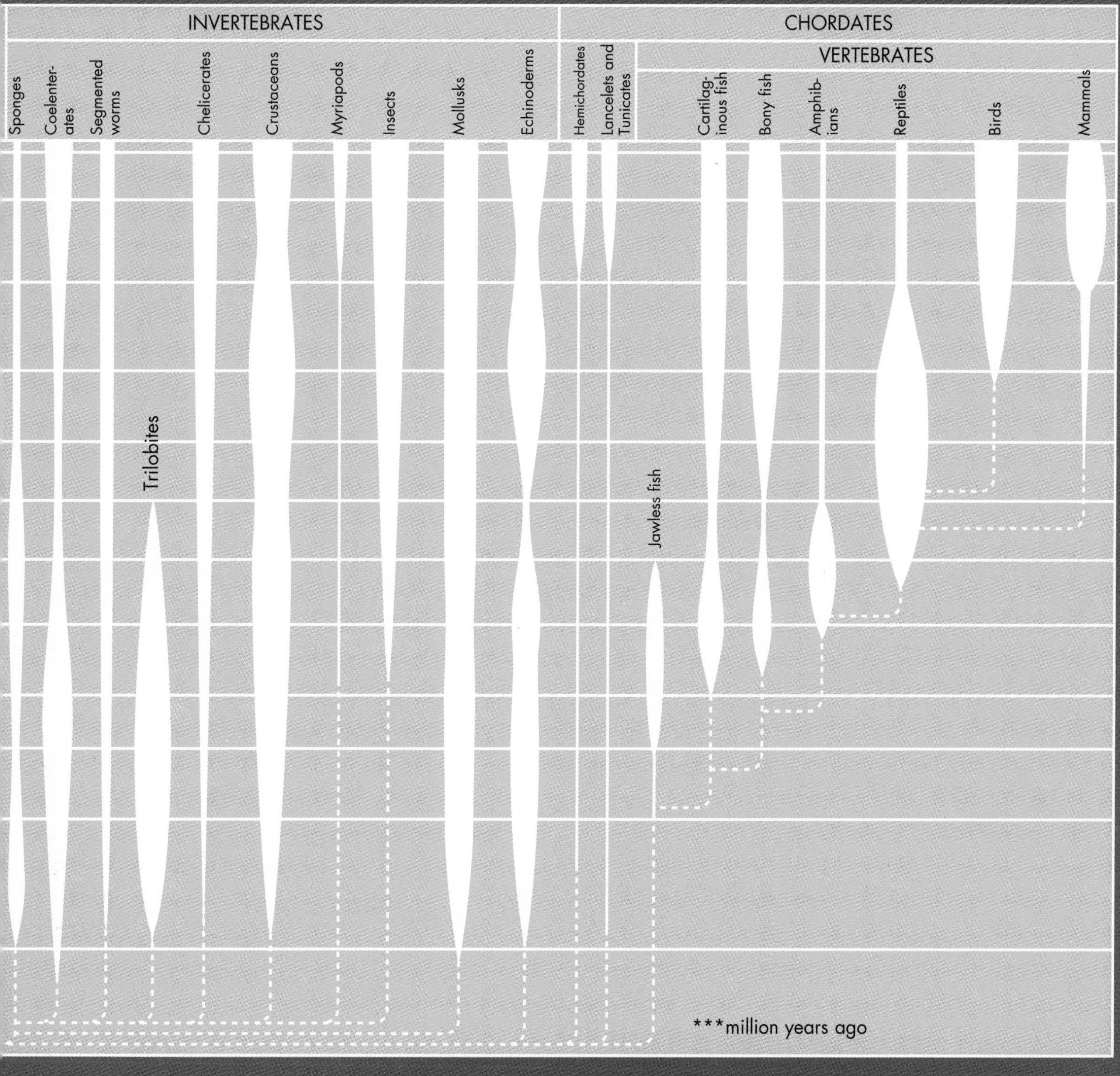

INVERTEBRATES

CHORDATES

VERTEBRATES

Sponges

Coelenter-ates

Segmented worms

Chelicerates

Crustaceans

Myriapods

Insects

Mollusks

Echinoderms

Hemichordates

Lancelets and Tunicates

Cartilag-inous fish

Bony fish

Amphib-ians

Reptiles

Birds

Mammals

Trilobites

Jawless fish

***million years ago